The woman's yoga book
For Beginners a Step-By-Step Picture

Finally, an Easy Way to Harness the Power of Yoga and Get the Dream Body You Deserve.

Let's Begin

TABLE OF CONTENTS

INTRODUCTION
HOW YOGA HELPS WITH WEIGHT LOSS
IS YOGA FOR ME?
A SHORT GUIDE TO A SUCCESSFUL YOGA PRACTICE

- When To Practice
- Where To Practice
- Eating & Drinking
- Yoga Gear
- How To Practice

YOGA POSES FOR WEIGHT LOSS

- Warm-Up Poses - Warming Up The Body & Calming The Mind
- Sun Salutations – Slimming & Detoxing The Body
- Standing Sequence Poses - Slimming Legs and Toning Arms
- Balancing Sequence Poses - Strengthening The Core Muscles & Improving Concentration
- Sitting Sequence Poses - Improving Flexibility & Stimulating Digestion
- Prone & Knees Sequence Poses - Melting Away Belly Fat & Shaping Buttocks
- Supine Sequence Poses - Building The Abdominal & Spinal Power
- Closing Sequence Poses - Relaxing The Body & Calming The Mind

Introduction

Unsightly flab. Battered self-esteem. Clothes that just don't fit anymore. Fighting the battle of the bulge is no walk in the park, and it's a problem that haunts many of us throughout our lives.

So how do we deal with it? It's often the same old story: you pick a diet fad, and spend weeks or months stomaching tasteless or downright weird food for breakfast, lunch and dinner. Then you sign up at your local gym, and torture yourself with exercise regimens that remind you of medieval punishment.

You might even drop by a pharmacy and stock up on weight loss pills (and peel off the labels when you get home, just so you're not reminded of the side effects).

You lose a few pounds here and there, until you realize you can't keep up with the extreme diet-exercise-pill lifestyle. Then you give up, and you pack the pounds right back on in a matter of weeks. Just like a yo-yo, you're back at square one.

This, in a nutshell, is why more and more people have searched for–and found–a better way. The practice of yoga is an **alternative weight loss method** that eliminates the pain, frustration and temporary results of dieting, and instead gives you profound and lasting change in an enjoyable and natural way.

In this book I'll guide you through the most important poses from traditional Hatha Yoga that aid in enhancing weight loss.

<u>**Yoga poses**</u> (also called **Asanas**) are physical postures that exercise your entire body, stretch and tone the muscles and joints, the spine and entire skeletal system. They have a beneficial effect not only on the body frame, but also on the internal organs, glands and nerves, keeping all systems healthy.

- <u>**Asanas reduce stress, enhance relaxation and revitalize body, mind and spirit.**</u>

On the following pages you'll find a detailed description of **86 Slimming Yoga Poses.** Every pose is illustrated with professional pictures and includes step-by-step instructions on how to assume the pose as well as its benefits and precautions. To make your studying easier, all poses are organized in groups: Sun Salutation, Standing Poses, Balancing Poses, Sitting Poses, etc.

Keep in mind that with the right guidance, harnessing the slimming power of yoga is easy (and a whole lot of fun too). This guide is packed with structured exercises, insights and instructions to help you start losing weight the enlightened way in just 15 – 30 minutes a day. And it doesn't matter how fit, experienced or old you are, because this book is designed for maximum ease of use and accessibility.

All you need to start your journey towards a slimmer, healthier and sexier you is an open mind and a desire for positive change. Remember, yoga is about progress, not perfection. Keep practicing and you will slowly perfect your postures, and this book will be your best friend along the way

I believe in you and I'm here to support you every step of the way.

Xoxo and deep breaths

How Yoga Helps With Weight Loss

It's no secret that three of the most common causes of weight problems are: lack of exercise, excessive or emotional eating and stress.

Losing weight successfully and permanently always boils down to finding **effective, safe** and **sustainable** solutions to these challenges— and this is where the ancient science of yoga comes in.

To the uninitiated, this may seem surprising. How is it possible that an unassuming set of low-impact stretches, techniques and exercises can be one of the most effective and permanent weight loss methods in the world?

> ☐ **The answer lies in yoga's 3-part approach to weight loss.**

Dieting alters your food intake. Exercise helps you tone and burn calories. Weight loss supplements manipulate the chemicals in your body. Most weight loss methods target just one area of weight loss, but yoga acts as a "one-stop-shop" by holistically targeting three primary areas:

1. EXERCISE

THE TYPICAL PROBLEM: Sure, you can spend a few weeks or months hauling yourself to the gym and exhausting your body with strenuous and repetitive exercise, but it's just a matter of time before you realize the results don't justify the effort, and you start replacing your torturous treadmill sessions with ache-free movies and snacks on the sofa.

YOGA'S SOLUTION: Yoga is a gentle form of exercise that helps you lose weight, detoxify and energize yourself. It focuses on gradual progress and teaches you to listen to your body, so you rarely suffer from strains, sprains or exhaustion. It gives you a full body workout, tones your muscles (without making you look like a body builder) and leaves you feeling rejuvenated instead of tired.

Yoga practice never gets boring, because there are hundreds of different poses to choose from, from beginner poses to advanced sequences. Plus, since you don't need any equipment, you can stop braving the traffic and cancel your gym membership.

☐ **Unlike diets, yoga gives you long-term rewards.**

A two-year study by the University of Otago in New Zealand found that women who followed a program of Yoga and meditation were successful in losing weight and keeping it off, while those who focused on dieting did not

2. THE MIND-BODY CONNECTION

THE TYPICAL PROBLEM: You crave unhealthy food just a little too often, you perhaps indulge in bad habits like snacking, overeating or drinking, and you never seem to get enough sleep. You know what you're supposed to do to take care of your body, but you often allow your cravings and impulses to get the best of you. Why is it so hard to do the right thing?

YOGA'S SOLUTION: Yoga gives you a direct line to your body and its needs. The connection begins on the yoga mat when you are trained to be aware of your breathing and of every part of your body. This results in a heightened mind-body connection in your everyday life, which in turn translates to better choices.

Your stop craving unhealthy food, you don't overeat and you eat to nourish yourself instead of just to kill hunger. You stay away from bad lifestyle habits because you're constantly mindful of the damage they can do to your body. When you're tired, you adhere to your body's signs and get sufficient rest. The result is a happier, healthier, slimmer you.

☐ **It's not just what you eat, it's how you eat it!**

Yoga teaches you to eat slowly and mindfully, so your body can absorb nutrients more efficiently. In a revealing study, Dr. Kathleen

Melanson from the University of Rhode Island found that a group of women instructed to eat a plate of pasta slowly ended up consuming 67 less calories as compared to when they wolfed down the exact same meal quickly. A normal person doing this 3 times a day for breakfast, lunch and dinner would save themselves 201 calories a day, or 1,407 calories a week–which is enough to lose 17 – 22 pounds in a year.

3. RELAXATION

THE TYPICAL PROBLEM: You constantly wish there were just a few extra hours every day so you can get more things done, or at least get some time to yourself. Your various responsibilities pull you in a hundred different directions, and you often feel stressed, frustrated and helpless. You often attempt to relieve your stress with unhealthy habits like binge eating or skipping sleep, which end up doing you more harm than good.

YOGA'S SOLUTION: Yoga exercises and techniques are designed to elevate your consciousness and guide you into a deep state of relaxation, where even the most stubborn stress melts away like butter in a microwave.

Unlike other forms of exercise, it strengthens not only your body, but also your mind and soul, leaving you empowered to make healthy lifestyle choices and triumph over the rigors of life.

Whenever you feel overwhelmed by stress or you just need a pick-me-up, you can retreat to a quick yoga session for an instant and lasting sensation of calmness, bliss and overall wellbeing.

☐ **Stress makes you fat!**

A survey by the American Psychological Association found that 4 in 10 Americans attempt to manage stress by overeating or eating unhealthy food, which in turn leads to weight problems.

Is Yoga For Me?

I get asked this question all the time. There's a common misconception out there that Yoga is an extreme religious practice, which makes many people scared to even try it! So before we go any further, let me make this very clear.

Yoga is a holistic physical, mental and spiritual practice that originated in India, but it doesn't mean it's only for bearded men meditating in caves. Millions of people across the world use it for a variety of purposes, such as stress-relief, healing, mental and spiritual clarity, and of course weight loss.

Yoga does **NOT** require you to give up the things you love, so you can still do, eat, drink and experience the joys of modern life.

Yoga is **NOT** a religion, it's a form of exercise, so you don't have to adopt any crazy beliefs, and you don't have to give up any beliefs you already have.

Yoga will **NOT** take up much of your time at all… so you can still make time for it no matter how busy or stressed you are.

Trust me—**anyone can do Yoga!** I'm just a normal city girl. I live in an apartment, I run a business, I have a wonderful husband and son, and I enjoy partying, eating out, movies, music and traveling as much as anyone else! Yet still, by investing just a little time into discovering the secrets of Yoga, I was able to get the body, health and happiness that contemporary diet and slimming plans were never able to give me. I've started teaching Yoga classes in my neighborhood, and my students enjoy the exact same results I have!

More and more busy executives, Hollywood celebrities and everyday folks are integrating 15-minute yoga sessions into their lives, and reaping the rewards—while still doing, eating and believing in what they like!

A Short Guide To A Successful Yoga Practice

IMPORTANT! If you have a medical condition you should consult your medical or health specialist before practicing any of the poses included in this book. It also applies to pregnant women and children below 12 years old.

The information provided within this book is believed to be accurate based on the personal experience of the authors but the reader is responsible for consulting with their own health professional before changing the diet or starting an exercise program; it is not a substitute for proper medical advice.

When To Practice

Put aside a specific time in your day to enjoy your yoga practice. Dawn and dusk are considered the best times of the day to practice yoga, as the rising and setting of the sun charge our body with special energy. However, if these times are impossible for you, find another time of the day that works best for you and practice consistently.

Practice in the **morning** if you want to prepare your mind and body for the day, and charge your body with positive energy. Keep in mind that in the morning or in cold weather your muscles will be stiffer, so ease carefully into the postures at first.

Practice in the **evening** if you want to relax after a stressful day, unwind and center. In the evenings your body will be more flexible, so you'll be able to go deeper into postures.

Where To Practice

Find a place where you are least likely to be disturbed. It can be your room, garden or beach - indoors or outdoors, wherever there is an even, flat surface.

If you are practicing indoors, make sure that the room is ventilated and with comfortable temperature. Air-conditioned rooms are not advisable - when the environment is cold your body is stiff, and muscles stretch slowly. A clean environment and fresh air adds additional benefits to the breathing practice.

Make sure that you have enough space to allow you to move around, and extend the arms and legs freely. Turn your phone off and hang a note on your door to say that you are having time to yourself. **This is YOUR time.**

Eating & Drinking

Never practice directly after eating. yoga should be done on empty stomach. Therefore allow at least 1 hour after a snack and 2 - 3 hours after a heavy meal before you begin your practice.

It is best to drink before or after your yoga session, to avoid becoming dehydrated. Try to avoid drinking water during the practice, to avoid losing your concentration on yoga postures and breathing.

However if you are practicing in the morning, have at least a glass of warm water before your practice, or a light snack (fruit or yoghurt). When you finish your practice eat a proper breakfast.

Yoga Gear

Wear comfortable, light, loose clothing, preferably made of natural fibers. Your clothes should not restrict your movements. Remove your jewelry, watch and spectacles if possible. Yoga is practiced with bare feet.

Get a special yoga mat for yourself. It provides padding as well as a non-slip surface to practice on, and makes your practice easier and safer. You can find one in any sports shop. No one else should use your mat. This is not only for hygiene reasons, but also because you will eventually build up energy on your mat that will support you throughout the yoga practice.

You can also get a **cushion** to make your meditation more comfortable and a **blanket** if you wish to cover yourself while relaxing in the Corpse Pose at the end of the session.

If you want, you can play relaxing, soothing **music** in the background - just make sure it's not too loud.

How To Practice

1) Perform all the postures **slowly and with control.** You are not in competition with anyone, not even yourself. You'll progress faster when you take things slowly.

2) **Concentrate on your breathing**, feel the air slowly flowing through your body, relaxing and energizing it.

3) **Relax**. Let go of any unnecessary tension, stress or negative thoughts.

4) Start every session with the **warm-up.** It's essential to avoid injuries.

5) **Modify the postures for your body.** The instructions and pictures of the yoga postures in this book are the final goal - the direction you are going towards, not where you need to be after your first few sessions. Experiment and explore different positions and alignments to make the posture work for your body.

6) **Don't expect instant results.** Yoga is a not a quick fix for your weight problems. Patience is a key to unlocking the long-term slimming benefits of yoga.

7) **Have Fun!** The best way to get results with your yoga practice is to enjoy it. Feeling happy while practicing yoga puts the mind and body into a positive state.

8) Most Importantly, listen to and respect your body. Never force any movement. **Let your body lead you, it is your greatest teacher!**

Yoga Poses For Weight Loss

Warm-Up Poses - Warming Up The Body & Calming The Mind

UPPER BODY TWISTS

Stand straight with your legs wide apart and hands resting on the side of your body. Inhale and raise the hands up from the sides to the shoulder level. Exhale and turn your upper body to the left keeping the arms and shoulders straight. Turn as far as possible, feeling the gentle twist in your lower back and abdominal muscles. Inhale and twist back to the front. Exhale and twist to the right side. Repeat.

FORWARD AND BACK BENDS

Stand straight with your legs wide apart. Inhale and rest your hands on your waist. Exhale and bend forward from the waist keeping the knees straight. Inhale and come back up. Exhale and bend backward, pulling your shoulders and elbows to the back. Repeat.

SIDE BENDS

Stand straight with your legs wide apart, straight knees. Inhale and rest your hands on your waist. Exhale and bend to the left side, keep your back straight as if it was glued to the wall. Inhale and come back up. Exhale and repeat on the other side.

UPPER BODY ROTATION

Stand straight with your legs wide apart. Inhale and bring your hands together above the head. Exhale and bend forward keeping the knees straight and palms together. Inhale and rotate your upper body to the left, continue inhaling and rotate to the back. Exhale and rotate to the right, continue exhaling and bend forward. Inhale and repeat the rotation in the opposite direction.

SHOULDERS ROTATION

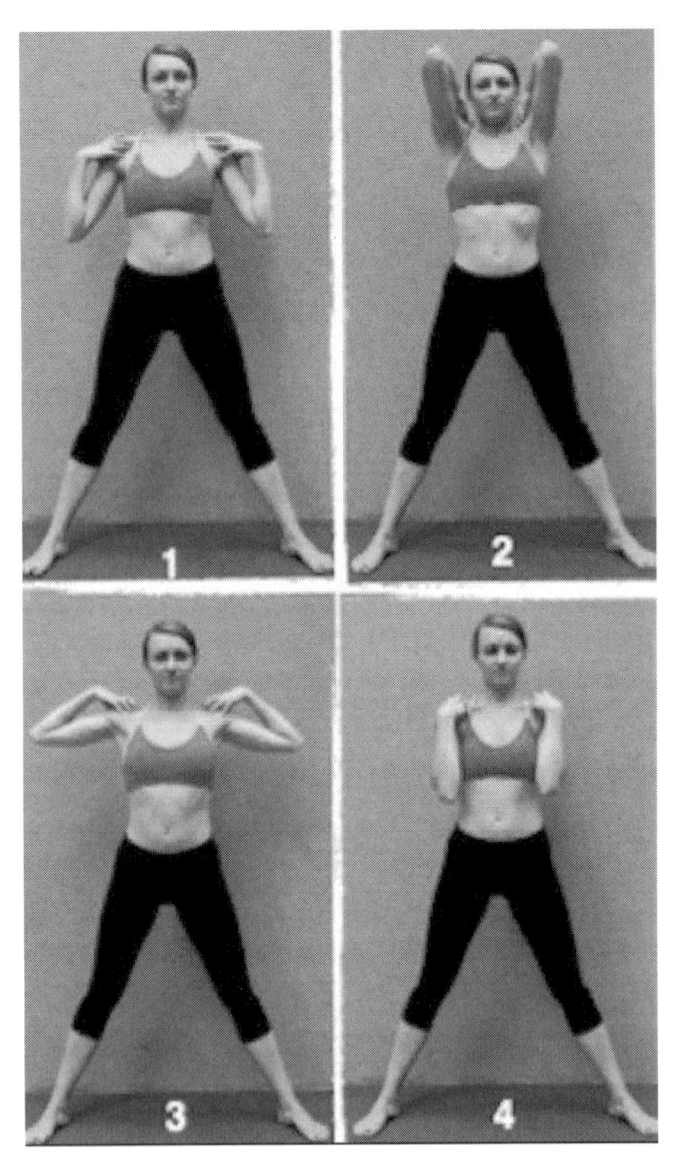

Stand straight with your legs wide apart. Bring your palms on the shoulders. Breathe normally. Rotate your arms in big circles to the back (5 circles). Repeat rotation to the front – (5 circles). Repeat.

WRISTS ROTATION

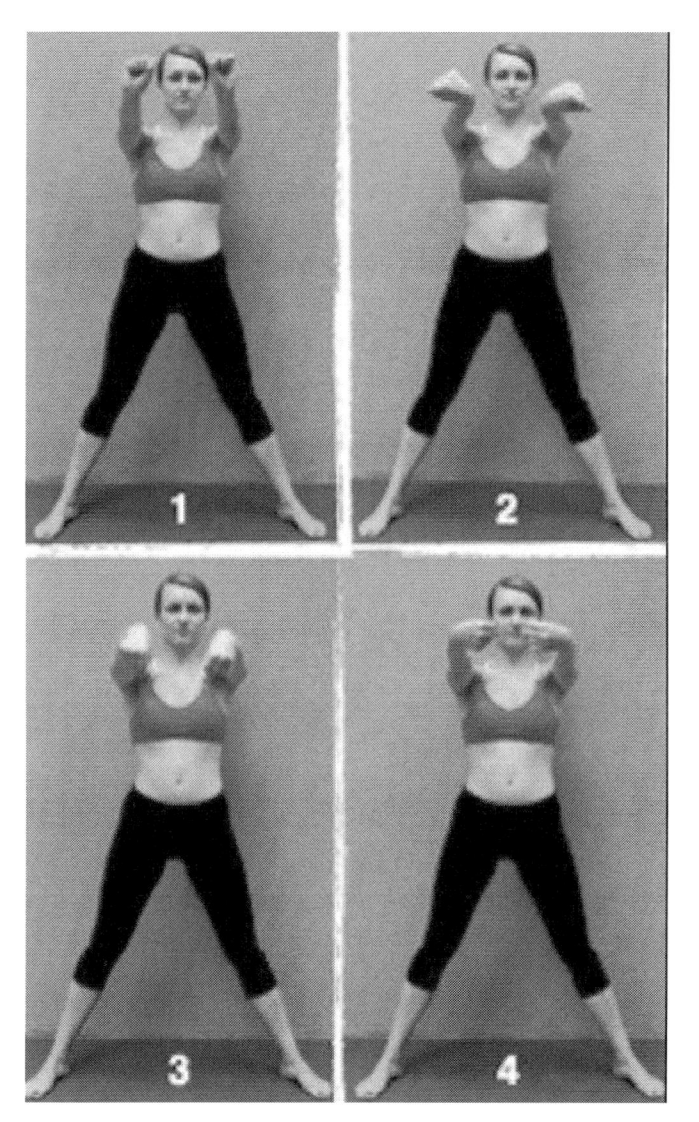

Stand straight with your legs wide apart. Bring your hands forward on the shoulder level. Rotate your both wrists, 5 circles in each direction.

HEAD ROTATION

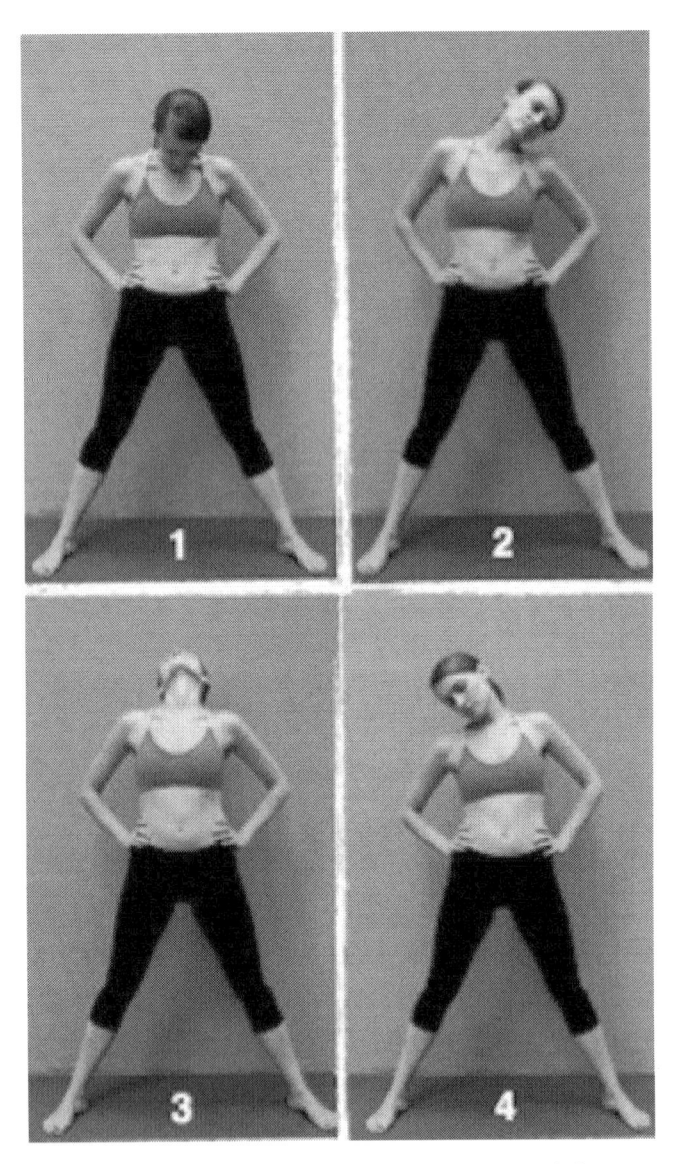

Stand straight with your legs wide apart. Bring your palms on the waist. Drop your head forward and slowly start rotating to the left, to the back, to the right and front. Repeat in the opposite direction.

FORWARD SWING

Stand straight with your legs wide apart. Raise your hands over the head, interlock the fingers and keep the elbows straight. Bend forward and swing the trunk down. Allow the arms and head to swing through the legs. Be tension free like a rag doll. Return smoothly to the upright position with the arms raised. Inhale forcefully through the nose while raising the arms up and exhale forcefully while swinging down. Repeat 10 times. It's a great exercise to clear lungs.

Sun Salutations – Slimming & Detoxing The Body

Sun Salutations are easily one of the most effective weight loss tools I learned while studying yoga in India. My Guru himself swore by this exercise, and credited some of his biggest weight loss success stories to it. Why? Because Sun Salutations…

- Build up the heat in your body, which dramatically speeds up your body's metabolism and fat burning efficiency.
- Burn fat when practiced in a fast pace.
- Stimulate and balance all systems in your body, including the digestive system.
- Strengthen the back and balances your metabolism.

Best of all, the Sun Salutation is really easy to do (no acrobatic moves here!). Keep in mind that the practice should be immediately discontinued if fever, acute inflammation, boils or rashes occur due to excess toxins in the body. When the toxins have been eliminated, the practice may be resumed.

PRECAUTIONS

Sun Salutations shouldn't be practiced by people with high blood pressure, coronary artery disorders or by those who have had a stroke, as it may over stimulate or damage a week heart or blood vessel system. It should also be avoided in case of hernia and intestinal tuberculosis. People with back conditions such as slipped disc and sciatica should consult a doctor before the practice. Women should avoid it during the onset of menstruation; practice can be resumed towards the end of the period.

SUN SALUTATIONS SEQUENCE POSES

PRAYER POSE

Come to the front of your mat. Stand straight with your legs together, tuck in your tailbone, palms on the chest. Breathe normally.

STANDING BACK BEND

Inhale and raise your both hands up above the head, slightly bend to the back looking upwards.

FORWARD BEND

Exhale and bend forward. Touch the floor with your fingers or palms (go as far as your flexibility allows you). Bring the forehead as close to the knees as possible. Don't strain your back and keep the knees straight.

HALF COBRA POSE

Place your palms on the floor beside the feet and keep the arms straight. Inhale, lift your head up and bring your left leg to the back, drop your left knee on the floor and bend your right knee. In the final pose, the left foot, both hands, left knee and toes support the body. The back is slightly arched and the head faces forward. Look upwards.

PLANK POSE

Hold the breath and from Half Cobra Pose bring your right leg back, straighten your knees and hands, palms directly below the shoulders. Drop the hips until the body forms a straight line from the top of your head to your heels. Look forward.

ASHTANGA POSE

Exhale and from Plank Pose lower your knees, chest and chin on the floor. Keep your elbows close to your body. In the final position only the toes, knees, chest, palms and chin (8 parts of the body) should touch the floor. The buttocks, hips and abdomen should be raised above the mat.

COBRA POSE

Inhale, keep your hands beside your chest, elbows close to your body and slide the chest forward raising the head and shoulders, then, straightening the elbows. Arch the back into the Cobra Pose, look up and relax your neck and shoulders. This will lower the hips and the buttocks to the floor.

DOWNWARD DOG POSE

Hold the breath, raise your hips up and lower the head between the arms so that the back and legs form two sides of a triangle. Keep the knees and hands straight. Push the heels and head towards the floor.

HALF COBRA POSE

Hold the breath and from Downward Facing Dog lean forward and bring your left leg forward. Place your palms on the floor beside the left foot and keep the arms straight. Drop your right knee on the floor and bend your left knee. The back is slightly arched and the head faces forward, look upwards.

FORWARD BEND

Exhale and from the Half Cobra Pose bring your right leg forward. Bend forward and touch the floor with your fingers or palms (go as far as your flexibility allows you). Bring the forehead as close to the knees as possible. Don't strain your back and keep the knees straight.

BACK BEND

Inhale and raise your both hands up above the head, slightly bend to the back looking upwards.

PRAYER POSE

Exhale and release your hands, bring the palms to the chest. Stand straight with your legs together, tuck in your tailbone. Breathe normally.

Standing Sequence Poses- Slimming Legs and Toning Arms

ONE LEG FORWARD BEND

Stand straight with legs together. Bring your left leg forward; turn your right foot to 45 degrees. Bring your both palms together behind your back, interlock the fingers and place your palms on your lower back. Inhale raise your head up, expand your chest and look up. Exhale and bend forward, bringing your forehead as close as possible to the knee, while keeping both legs straight. Stay in this pose for 5 breaths and with inhale raise up back to the starting pose. Repeat on the other side.

Precautions: people with weak heart or lower back problems should not practice this posture

Benefits: opening hips and shoulders, stretching the lower back, contracting abdominal muscles, helping to burn abdominal fat, strengthening the legs.

TRIANGLE POSE

Stand straight with legs together. Bring your left leg forward and turn your right foot to 45 degrees. Inhale, stretch the arms sideways on the shoulder level so that they are in one straight line. Exhale, bend to the left, bringing left hand down to the left foot and right hand up. Keep your knees straight and arms in straight line. Imagine that the front of your body is glued to the wall forming one straight surface. Look up at the left hand in the final position and hold the position for 5 breaths. Inhale, return to the upright position with the arms in a straight line. Exhale, release the hands on the sides of your body. Repeat on the other side.

Precautions: None

Benefits: toning the waist muscles and the back of the legs, improving digestion, reducing waistline fat

ONE HAND BACKBEND

Stand straight with legs together. Bring your left leg forward; turn your right foot to 45 degrees. Inhale, stretch the arms sideways on the shoulder level so that they are in one straight line. Exhale, tilt your upper body to the back, bringing left hand up, right hand stays on the leg. Keep your knees straight. Look up at the left hand in the final position and hold the position for 5 breaths. Inhale, return to the starting position with the arms in a straight line. Exhale, release the hands to the sides of your body. Repeat on the other side.

Precautions: make sure that you perform this pose very slowly, otherwise you might feel dizzy

Benefits: toning the waist muscles and the back of the legs, improving digestion, reducing waistline fat

REVOLVED TRIANGLE

Stand straight with the feet more than shoulder width apart. Turn the left foot to the left side. Inhale, raise the arms sideways to the shoulder level. Exhale, twist the trunk to the left, bend forward and

bring your right hand on the outer side of the left foot and the left hand up, stretched vertically so that both arms are forming a straight line. Look up at the left hand and keep your knees straight. Hold the final position for 5 breaths, balancing the body and feeling the twist and stretch of the back. Inhale, raise your hands up to shoulder level. Exhale, return to the center position. Repeat on the other side.

Option: If you can't place your hand on the outer side of the foot, you can place your palm on your ankle or calf - just remember to keep the knees straight.

Precautions: People suffering from back conditions should avoid this posture

Benefits: toning the thigh, calf, hip and hamstring muscles, reducing fat around the waist and hips, strengthening and toning the arms

SIDE ANGLE POSE

Stand straight with the feet more than shoulder width apart. Turn the left foot to the left side. Inhale, bend your left knee and place your left elbow on the thigh, lean forward, so that you left thigh is parallel to the floor. Exhale, extend your right arm over the ear until you form a straight line from the tips of your fingers to the toes. Look to your right side and hold the pose for 5 breaths. Inhale, release the right hand to the back. Exhale, return to the starting position. Repeat on the other side.

Precautions: People with weak heart and lower back problems should avoid this posture.

Benefits: toning ankles, knees and thighs, reducing fat around the waist and hips, toning the legs

REVOLVED SIDE ANGLE POSE

Stand erect with the feet widely spread apart. Inhale, turn the left foot to the left side. Exhale, bend your left knee, lean forward, rotate your trunk, bring your palms together and place your right elbow on the outer side of your left knee. Expand your chest up. Hold this pose

for 5 breaths. Inhale, release the hands to the front. Exhale, return to the starting position. Repeat on the other side.

Precautions: People suffering from serious back conditions and weak knees shouldn't practice this posture

Benefits: Improving digestion, helping to remove waste matter from the colon without strain

CHEST EXPAND

Stand erect with the feet widely spread apart. Inhale, raise your both hands up and tilt to the back. Expand the chest and hold it for few seconds. Exhale, release the hands and return to the starting position.

Precautions: People with weak heart and lower back problems should not practice this posture

Benefits: Stretching arms and spine, helping in deep breathing, toning abdominal muscles, strengthening the lower back, calves and buttocks

WIDE LEG FORWARD BEND 1

Stand erect with the feet widely spread apart. Inhale, raise your both hands up, tilt to the back and expand the chest. Exhale, bend forward, place your palms on the floor and slowly push your head

towards the floor. Hold the posture for 5 breaths. Inhale, slowly raise your head and hands up. Exhale, release the hands and return to the starting position.

Option: If you can't touch your head to the floor, just bring your hands on the floor - don't strain, go only as far as your body allows you

Precautions: People with serious neck/arm/shoulder problems should not practice this posture

Benefits: Strengthening and slimming the arms and upper back, stretching the hamstrings

WIDE LEG FORWARD BEND 2

Stand erect with the feet widely spread apart. Inhale, bring the hands to the back, and interlock the fingers. Exhale, bend forward and raise your hands up, so that the shoulder blades are coming closer. Hold the posture for 5 breaths. Inhale, slowly drop your hands on the lower

back and raise your head up. Exhale, release the hands and return to the starting position.

Precautions: People with serious neck/arm/shoulder problems should not practice this posture

Benefits: strengthening and relieving stiffness in shoulders, arms and upper back, stretching the hamstrings

WIDE LEG FORWARD TWIST

From the Wide Leg Forward Bend I leave your left hand in the center on the floor and with inhale twist your trunk and raise your right hand up. Both hands should form a straight line. Look up. Hold the pose for

5 breaths. Exhale, bring your left hand back on the floor. Repeat on the right side

Precautions: People with serious neck/arm/shoulder problems should not practice this posture

Benefits: strengthening the arms, shoulders, chest and upper back, toning the abdominal muscles and lower back

WARRIOR 1

Stand straight with legs together. Bring your left leg forward, turn your right foot to 45 degrees. Bend your left knee so that thigh is

parallel to the floor but remember not to bring the knee beyond the ankle (it should be just above the ankle). Inhale and raise your both hands up, stretch the spine and gaze forward. Hold the pose for 5 long breaths. Exhale and release your hands down, go back to the starting pose. Repeat on the other side.

Precautions: People with weak heart and lower back problems should not practice this posture

Benefits: it relieves stiffness in shoulders and back, tones up the ankles and knees and cures stiffness of he neck, it reduces fat around the hips, it helps with deep breathing.

WARRIOR 2

Stand straight with legs together. Bring your left leg forward, turn your right foot to 45 degrees. Bend your left knee so that thigh is parallel to the floor. Inhale and stretch your hands sideways on the shoulder level and gaze at your left palm. Your right knee remains straight. The left knee should not extend beyond the ankle but should be in line with the heel. Hold the pose for 5 long breaths. Exhale and release your hands down, go back to the starting pose. Repeat on the right side.

Precautions: People with weak heart and lower back problems should not practice this posture

Benefits: legs muscles become shapely and stronger, bringing elasticity to the legs and back muscles and also toning the abdominal organs, strengthening the arms

EASY WARRIOR 3

From Warrior 1, exhale lower your left knee and bend the trunk forward. Rest the chest on the thigh and bring your hands forward. Keep the arms straight and the palms together. Hold this position for 5 long breaths. Exhale, lower your hands to the knee and raise up while straightening your both legs. Go back to starting position. Repeat on the right side.

Precautions: People with weak heart and lower back problems should not practice this posture

Benefits: contracting and toning abdominal organs and making the leg muscles more shapely and sturdy; helping to get rid of fat in abdominal area and hips; strengthening the thighs

EASY HALF MOON POSE

From Easy Warrior Pose 3 place your palms on the floor beside the feet, keep the arms straight. Inhale, raise your right leg up, hold it parallel to the floor and straighten your left knee. Look down on the floor. Hold the posture for 5 breaths. Exhale, drop your right leg on the floor and go back to the starting pose. Repeat on the other side.

Precautions: People with lower back problems should not practice this posture.

Benefits: reducing fat around the hips; stretching the hamstrings, calf and thigh muscles; toning the buttocks

Balancing Sequence Poses - Strengthening The Core Muscles & Improving Concentration

TREE POSE

Stand with the feet together and the arms by the sides of your body. Steady the body and distribute the weight equally on both feet. Raise your left leg, bend the knee and place the sole on the inner side of your right thigh. Fix your gaze on one point and find the balance. Inhale, raise the arms over the head, bring the palms together, relax your shoulders. Stretch the whole body from top to bottom, without losing balance or moving the feet. Hold the position for 5 breaths. Exhale slowly release the arms and left leg down to the starting position. Repeat on the other side.

Precautions: be careful with the ankles; warm it up before the practice

Benefits: developing physical and mental balance, stretching the abdominal muscles and the intestines, helping to keep the abdominal muscles and nerves toned, improving the posture

STANDING HALF BOW BALANCE

Stand with the feet together and focus your gaze on point. Inhale, bend the left knee and grab the ankle with the left hand behind the body, raise the right hand up. Keep both knees together and maintain the balance. Exhale, slowly raise and stretch the right leg backward as high as comfortable. Reach upward and forward with the right arm. Focus the gaze on a right palm. Hold the position for 5 breaths. Inhale, lower the right arm to the side, lower the left leg, bringing the knees together. Exhale, release the left ankle and lower the foot to the floor, lower the right arm to the side. Repeat on the other side

Precautions: People who suffer from a weak heart, high blood pressure, back problems, hernia, colitis, peptic or duodenal ulcers or vertigo should not practice it

Benefits: strengthening the back, shoulders, arms, hips and legs, developing a sense of balance and coordination and improving concentration

STANDING KNEE TO CHEST BALANCE

Stand with the feet together and the arms by the sides. Inhale, raise your left leg, grab hold of the shin and bring the knee close to the chest with toes pointing down. Stretch the whole body from top to bottom, without losing balance or moving the feet. Fix the gaze on one point and find the balance. Hold the position for 5 breaths. Exhale and slowly release the arms and left leg down to the starting position. Repeat on the other side.

Precautions: Be careful with the ankles, warm it up before the practice.

Benefits: developing physical and mental balance, stretching abdominal muscles and intestines, toning abdominal muscles and nerves, improving posture and strengthening arms, stimulating digestion

STANDING KNEE TO THE SIDE BALANCE

From the Standing Knee To Chest Balance inhale and bring your bent knee to the left side and your right hand to the right side on the shoulder level. Stretch the whole body from top to bottom, without losing balance or moving the feet. Fix the gaze on one point and find the balance. Hold the position for 5 breaths. Exhale, slowly release the left leg to the front and drop the foot on the floor. Release the right hand. Repeat on the other side.

Precautions: Be careful with the ankles, warm it up before the practice.

Benefits: developing physical and mental balance, stretching abdominal muscles and intestines, toning abdominal muscles and nerves, improving posture and strengthening arms, stimulating digestion

EAGLE POSE

Stand with the feet together and the arms by the sides. Hold the left leg straight, bend the right leg and wrap it around the left leg while bending your left knee. The right thigh should be in front of the left thigh and the top of the right foot should rest on the calf of the left leg. Bend the elbows and bring them in front of the chest. Inhale, wrap the right hand around the left hand. Place the palms together to resemble an eagle's beak. Keep the eyes focused on the fixed point. Hold the final position for 5 breaths, then raise the body, and release the legs and arms. Repeat on the other side

Precautions: People with tight knees should be careful with this posture

Benefits: strengthening the muscles and loosening the shoulders, arms and legs, stretching upper back, improving concentration.

CHAIR POSE

Stand with the feet together and the arms by the sides. Inhale, raise the arms over the head. Exhale, bend the knees and lower the trunk, breathe normally. Keep your back straight and hold the pose for 5

breaths. Inhale, straighten the legs. Exhale, lower the arms and come back to standing pose.

Precautions: People suffering from serious back conditions should avoid this posture

Benefits: removing stiffness in the shoulders, the ankles become strong and the leg muscles develop evenly, the diaphragm is lifted up and this gives a gentle massage to the heart, the abdominal organs and the back are toned and the chest is developed by being fully expanded

TIPTOE POSE

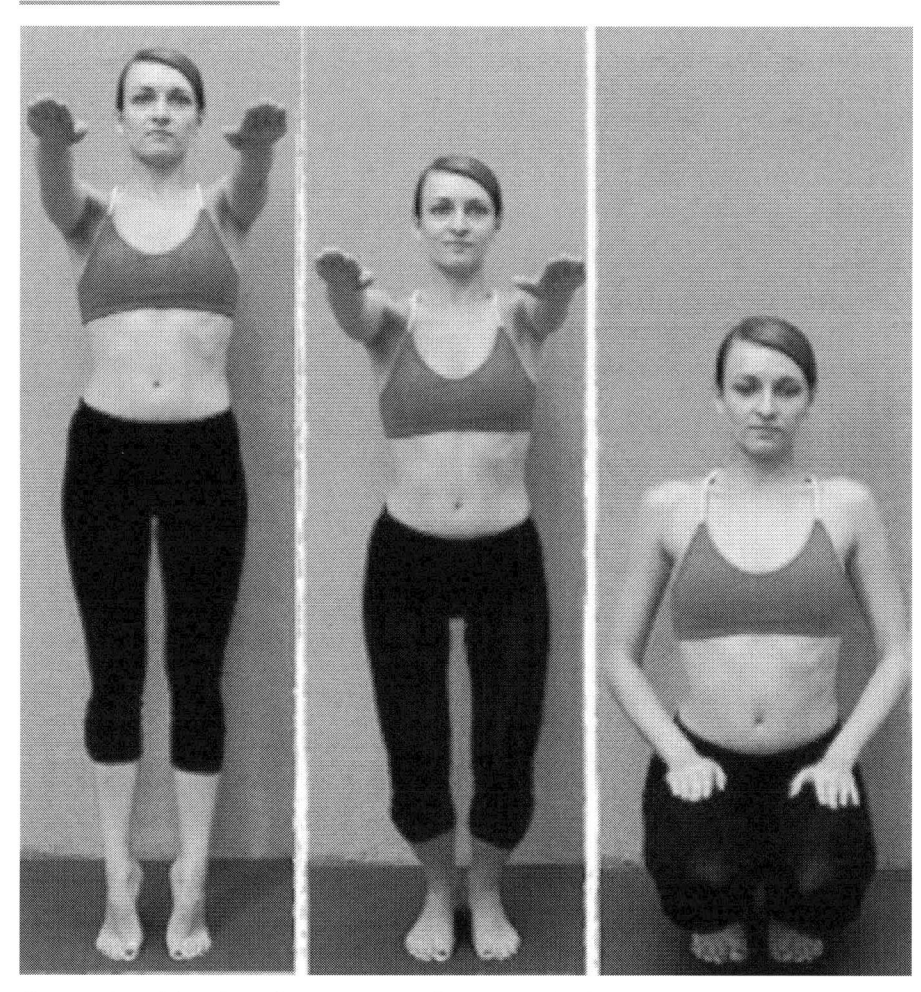

Stand with the feet together and the arms by the sides. Inhale, raise up on the toes and bring your hands to the front on the shoulder level. Exhale, squat while gazing at one point. Raise the heels and balance

on the tiptoes. Allow the knees to come forward slightly so that the thighs are parallel to the floor. Place your palms on the thighs, straighten your back and balance the whole body. Stay in this position for 5 breaths. release the pose, drop your knees on the floor and sit between your feet to relax.

Precautions: People with sciatica, slipped disc, ankle or knee problems should not practice this asana

Benefits: strengthening the toes, ankles, lower back and thighs, improving balance and concentration

Sitting Sequence Poses - Improving Flexibility & Stimulating Digestion

EASY MEDITATION POSE

Sit down with crossed legs. Place your hands on the knees. Close your eyes. Keep the head, neck and back upright and straight. Relax the whole body. Arms should be relaxed and not held straight

Precautions: People with severe knees problems should not be sitting in this posture for too long

Benefits: this is the easiest and most comfortable meditative pose; it facilitates mental and physical balance without strain or pain

HALF LOTUS POSE

Sit down with legs straight. Bend one leg and place the sole of the foot on the inside of the opposite thigh. Bend the other leg and place the foot on top of the opposite thigh. Without any strain, try to place the upper heel as near as possible to the abdomen. Adjust the position to feel comfortable. Place the hands on the knees and close your eyes. Keep the head, neck and back upright and straight. Relax the whole body. Arms should be relaxed and not held straight.

Precautions: People suffering from sciatica or weak or injured knees should not perform this posture

Benefits: allowing the body to be held completely steady for long periods of time, holding the trunk and head like a pillar with the legs as a firm foundation. Applying pressure to the lower spine, which has a relaxing effect on the nervous system. The breath becomes slow, muscular tension is decreased and blood pressure is reduced. The normally large blood flow of the legs is redirected to the abdominal region stimulating digestive process.

LOTUS POSE

Sit with legs straight in front of the body. Bend the left knee and place the left foot on the right thigh. Bend the right knee and place the right foot on the left thigh. Adjust the pose so that it is comfortable, the knees should be firmly on the floor. Place the hands on the knees and

close your eyes. Keep the head, neck and back upright and straight. Relax the whole body. Arms should be relaxed and not held straight.

Precautions: People with sciatica or sacral infections should not perform this posture

Benefits: It's a healthy position to sit in, especially for those suffering from varicose veins, tired and aching muscles or fluid retention in the legs. It increases the efficiency of the entire digestive system, relieving stomach ailments such as hyperacidity and peptic ulcer. You can practice Lotus Pose directly after meals, for at least 5 minutes to enhance the digestive function.

THUNDERBOLT POSE 1

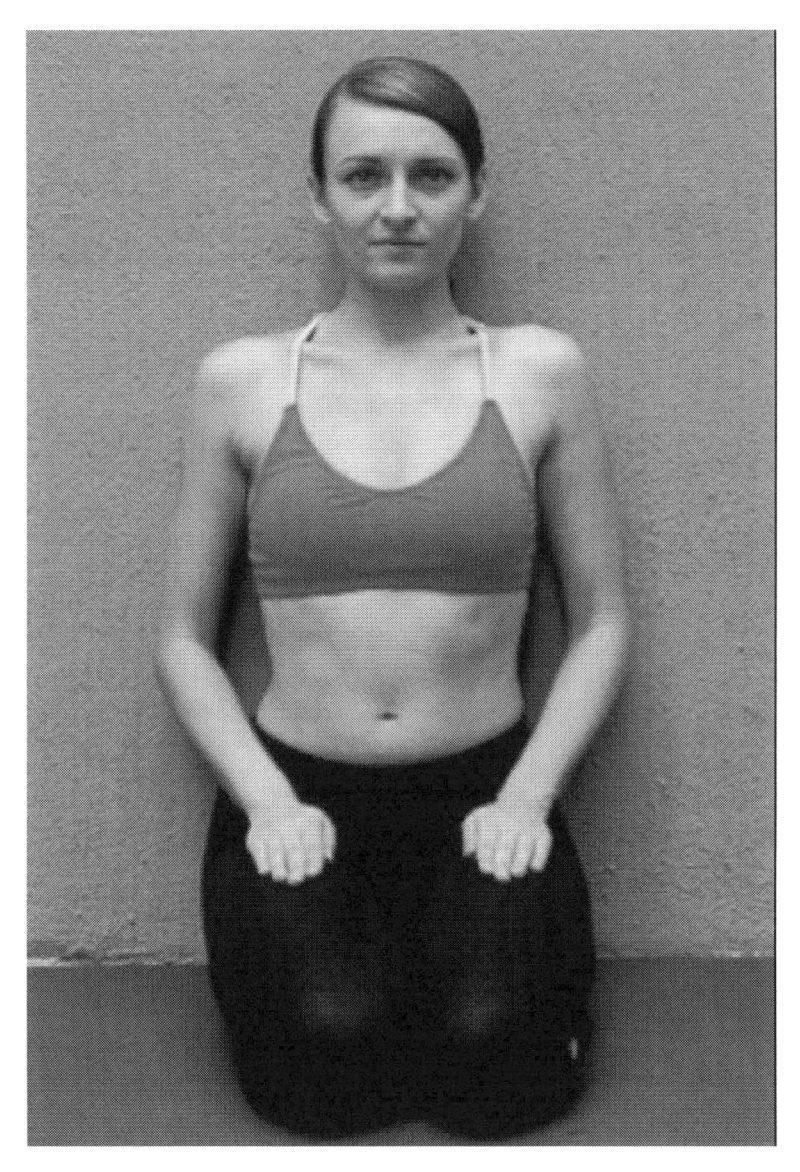

Kneel down on the floor with the knees close together. Bring the big toes together and separate the heels. Lower the buttocks onto the inside surface of the feet with the heels touching the sides of the hips. Place the hands on the thighs, palms down. The back and head should be straight but not tense. Close the eyes, relax the arms and the whole body.

Option: If there is a pain in the thighs or ankles, the knees may be separated slightly while maintaining the posture. You can also put the pillow below your buttocks and sit on it.

Precautions: Be careful with your ankles and knees

Benefits: Altering the flow of blood and nervous impulses into pelvic region and strengthening the pelvic muscles. Increasing the efficiency of the entire digestive system, relieving stomach ailments such as hyperacidity and peptic ulcer. This is the only posture that you can practice directly after meals, for at least 5 minutes to enhance the digestive function.

THUNDERBOLT POSE 2

From the Thunderbolt Pose 1 bring your hands to the back and interlock the fingers. Inhale, raise your head up and expand the chest. Exhale, bend forward and rest the chest on the thighs and forehead on the floor. Raise the palms up as high as you can, so that the shoulder blades will come closer to each other. Hold the pose for 5 breaths. Inhale drop the hands on your lower back and slowly raise the head and upper body up. Exhale, go back to the starting pose - place the hands on the thighs, palms down and look forward.

Option: If you have tight shoulders, you can just rest your hands on the lower back without raising it up

Precautions: Be careful with your ankles, knees and shoulders

Benefits: increasing the efficiency of the entire digestive system, relieving stomach ailments such as hyperacidity and peptic ulcer, stretching and strengthening the shoulders and arms

THUNDERBOLT POSE 3

From the Thunderbolt Pose 1 bring your left palm below the belly button, put the right palm on top of the left palm. Inhale, raise your head up and expand the chest. Exhale, bend forward and rest the chest on the thighs and forehead on the floor. Your palms are pressing the stomach. Hold the pose for 5 breaths. Inhale, slowly raise the head and upper body up. Exhale, go back to the starting pose - place the hands on the thighs, palms down and look forward.

Precautions: Be careful with your ankles and knees. People with gastric problems shouldn't perform it.

Benefits: Speeding up digestion due to the pressure on the stomach; getting rid of excess wind or gas in your belly adding strength to the calf and thigh muscles.

ONE LEG FORWARD BEND

Sit down with your legs wide apart. Inhale, raise your both hands up above the head. Exhale, twist the trunk and bend forward to the left leg. Grab hold of your left toe (or calf). Bring the forehead to the knee and keep the knee straight. Hold the pose for 5 breaths. Inhale, raise your both hands up above the head. Exhale and repeat on the other side.

Precautions: People suffering from slipped disc, sciatica or hernia should not practice this posture

Benefits: stretching hamstrings and increasing flexibility in the hips; toning and massaging the entire abdominal and pelvic region, slimming the abdominal area and stimulating circulation to the nerves and muscles of the spine.

ONE LEG FORWARD BEND 2

Sit down on the floor with your legs wide apart. Bring your left hand up and rest your right hand on the back. Twist your trunk and bend forward to your right leg, grab hold of your right toe (or calf) with your left hand. Inhale, raise your head up, look up. Exhale, bend forward and bring the forehead as close as possible to the knee. Keep both knees straight. Hold the pose for 5 breaths. Repeat the movement on the other side.

Precautions: People suffering from slipped disc, sciatica or hernia should not practice this posture

Benefits: stretching hamstrings and increasing flexibility in the hips; toning and massaging the entire abdominal and pelvic region, slimming the abdominal area and stimulating circulation to the nerves and muscles of the spine.

WIDE LEGS FORWARD BEND

Sit down on the floor with your legs wide apart. Inhale, raise the both hands up above the head. Exhale, bend forward and grab hold of your left toe with your left hand and right toe with your right hand. Try to bring your forehead to the floor in between the knees, keep both knees straight. Hold the pose for 5 breaths. Inhale, raise your both hands and head up. Exhale, release both hands on the floor next to the thighs.

Precautions: People suffering from slipped disc, sciatica or hernia should not practice this posture

Benefits: stretching hamstrings and increasing flexibility in the hips; toning and massaging the entire abdominal and pelvic region, slimming the abdominal area and stimulating circulation to the nerves and muscles of the spine.

TWO LEGS FORWARD BEND

Sit down on the floor with your legs outstretched, feet together. Inhale, raise your both hands up above the head. Exhale, bend forward, slide the hands down the legs and grab hold of your feet (alternative: ankles, calves). Bring your head as close as possible to the knees, keeping your knees straight. Hold the pose for 5 breaths. Inhale and raise both hands up. Exhale and release both hands.

Precautions: People suffering from slipped disc, sciatica or hernia should not practice this posture

Benefits: stretching hamstrings and increasing flexibility in the hips; toning and massaging the entire abdominal and pelvic region, slimming the abdominal area and stimulating circulation to the nerves and muscles of the spine.

TWISTED POSE 1

Sit down on the floor with your legs outstretched, feet together. Bend the left knee and place the foot on the floor. Inhale, raise your both hands up above the head. Exhale, turn the trunk to the right side and place the right palm behind the right buttock, and the left palm next to right thigh, with the fingers pointing to each other. Twist the head and trunk as far to the right as is comfortable, using the arms as levers, while keeping the spine upright and straight. The buttocks should remain on the floor. The right elbow may bend a little, but try to keep it straight. Look over right shoulder as far as possible without straining, feel the twist in the lower back. Hold the final position for 5 breaths. Inhale, straighten your head and raise both hands up above the head, re-center the trunk. Exhale, release the hands; repeat on the other side.

Precautions: People with back complaints should be careful with this posture

Benefits: stretching the spine, loosening the vertebrae and toning the nerves, alleviating backache, neck pain lumbago and mild forms of sciatica

TWISTED POSE 2

Sit down on the floor with your legs outstretched, feet together. Bend the right knee and place the foot on the floor next to your left knee. Inhale, raise your both hands up above the head. Exhale, turn the trunk to the right side and place the right palm behind the right

buttock, and the left palm on the right shoulder, left elbow is pressing against the right knee. Twist the head and trunk as far to the right as is comfortable, using the arms as levers, while keeping the spine upright and straight. The buttocks should remain on the floor. Look over the right shoulder as far as possible without straining, feel the twist in the lower back. Hold the final position for 5 breaths. Inhale, straighten your head and raise both hands up above the head, re-center the trunk. Exhale, release the hands, repeat on the other side.

Precautions: People with back complaints should be careful with this posture

Benefits: stretching the spine, loosening the vertebrae and toning the nerves, alleviating backache, neck pain lumbago and mild forms of sciatica

SITTING HALF BOAT POSE

Sit down on the floor with your legs outstretched, feet together. Inhale, bend the left knee, grab hold of your left foot (alternative: ankle, heel, calf) and stretch the leg up. Keep the back and knee straight and try to bring your leg as close as possible to the forehead

without straining your neck. Gaze at the big toe and hold the pose for 5 breaths. Exhale, slowly release the leg on the floor. Repeat on the other side.

Precautions: People with back complaints or a displaced coccyx should not practice this pose.

Benefits: rendering the hamstring muscles and improving hips flexibility; toning abdominal muscles; strengthening arms and spine muscles

TWISTED HALF BOAT STRETCH

From the Sitting Half Boat Pose inhale and grab the outer side of your left foot (option: ankle, heal, calf) with your right hand. Twist the trunk towards the left side, extend the left arm to the back at the shoulder level. Turn the head to the back and gaze over the left shoulder at your left palm. Keep your knees and back straight. Hold the pose for 5 breaths. Exhale, straighten your head and trunk, release your left hand and bring the left leg down on the floor. Repeat on the other side.

Precautions: People with back complaints or a displaced coccyx should not practice this pose.

Benefits: rendering the hamstring muscles and improving hips flexibility; toning abdominal muscles; strengthening arms and spine muscles; gentle twist of the lower back is strengthening lower back muscles.

HIP ROCKING

Sit down on the floor with the legs outstretched, feet together. Inhale, bend the left knee, grab hold of the left knee and ankle and bring the hip to the side. Straighten your back, and start rocking the hip to the left and right (movement reminds rocking of the baby). Rock the leg for 5 breaths. Slowly release the leg on the floor. Repeat on the other side.

Precautions: People with back complaints or a displaced coccyx should not practice this pose.

Benefits: opening and releasing tension in the hip; improving flexibility of the hip joints; toning abdominal muscles; strengthening the spine

BUTTERFLY POSE

Sit down on the floor with the legs outstretched, feet together. Inhale, pull in your feet and bring the soles of the feet together, as close as possible to your pelvis, let the knees fall out to the sides. Bounce the knees gently (like a butterfly flapping it's wings). Breath normally and keep bouncing the knees for the duration of 5 breaths. Release the legs and go back to the starting position

Precautions: People with sciatica or knee problems should not practice this pose.

Benefits: improving the flexibility in the groin and hips region; relieving the inner thigh muscles tension; removing tiredness from long hours of walking or standing; preparing the legs for other meditative postures.

COBBLER'S POSE

Sit down on the floor with the legs outstretched, feet together. Inhale, pull in your feet and place the soles of the feet together, as close as possible to your pelvis, let the knees fall out to the sides. Keep the spine and the neck straight. Inhale, grasp your feet, raise your head up and bend to the back. Exhale, bend forward and bringing your forehead all the way down to the big toes. Press the elbows against the thighs, bringing them closer to the floor. Hold the pose for 5 breaths. Inhale, raise the head and trunk up. Exhale, return to the starting pose.

Precautions: People with sciatica or knee problems should not practice this pose.

Benefits: improving the flexibility in the groin and hips region; relieving the inner thigh muscles tension; soothing the lower abdominal organs and helping the excretory system remove waste from the body.

Prone & Knees Sequence Poses - Melting Away Belly Fat & Shaping Buttocks

CHILD'S POSE

Kneel on the floor, touch your big toes together and sit in between your heels, (you can separate the knees). Inhale, look forward and stretch the back. Exhale, bend forward bringing the chest to the thighs and forehead on the floor. Bring your hands to the back and lay them down on the floor next to the hips (option: you can bring the hands in the front of the body as far as you can reach). Hold this position for 5 long breaths and relax. Inhale, raise your head and trunk up. Exhale and release the pose.

Precautions: People having diarrhea or knee injury should avoid this pose.

Benefits: gently stretching the hips, thighs and ankles; it's a restorative posture, it helps you relax, calm down, relieve stress and fatigue; restoring balance in the body and releasing tension in the back, shoulders, and chest; practice it after Sun Salutations and in between sequences

CAT STRETCH

Sit down in Thunderbolt Pose, raise the buttocks and stand on the knees. Lean forward and place the palms flat on the floor beneath the shoulders with the fingers facing forward. The hands should be in line with the knees; the arms and thighs should be perpendicular to the floor. Do not bend the arms at the elbows, keep the arms and thighs straight. Inhale, raise the head and depress the lower back. Exhale, arch your back and bring the chin to the chest. Repeat this movement 10 times.

Precautions: Be careful with your knees and neck

Benefits: improving flexibility of the neck, shoulders and spine; toning digestive system; massaging the spine and abdominal organs; relaxing for the lower back.

ALTERNATE LEG-HAND BALANCE

From the Cat Stretch Pose, inhale and raise the left hand and right leg up, parallel to the floor. Balance the body in the center, look forward. Hold the pose for 5 breaths. Exhale, release the left hand and right leg. Repeat on the other side.

Precautions: People with knees or lower back problems should avoid this practice.

Benefit: improving the flexibility of the spine and lower back; toning and shaping abdominal muscles; slimming effect on thighs, buttocks and arms.

TIGER POSE

Assume the starting position for Cat Stretch and look forward. Inhale, swing your left leg to the back and bring the head up. Exhale, bend the left knee and swing the leg forward, bring the knee as close as possible to the forehead. Repeat the movement 5 times. Practice on the other side.

Precautions: People with recent or chronic injuries of the back, hips or knees should avoid this posture

Benefits: exercising and loosening the back by bending it alternately in both directions, toning the spinal nerves; relieving sciatica and loosening up the legs and hip joints; stretching abdominal muscles, improving digestion and stimulating blood circulation; reducing weight from the hips and thighs.

DOWNWARD DOG

Assume the starting position for Cat Stretch and look forward. Inhale, tuck in your toes and raise your hips up. Lower the head between the arms so that the back and legs form two sides of a triangle. Keep the knees and hands straight, gaze on the floor. Push the heels and head towards the floor. Hold the pose for 5 breaths. Bring your knees down to the floor and release the pose.

Precautions: People with diarrhea, headache, high blood pressure or carpel tunnel syndrome should not practice this posture

Benefits: calming the brain and relieving stress; energizing the body; stretching the arms, shoulders, hamstrings and calves; slimming effect on arms and legs; improving digestion, relieving headache, insomnia, back pain and fatigue

RAISED LEG DOWNWARD DOG

From the Downward Dog Pose inhale, raise your left leg up, as high as possible, keep it straight. Press the palms evenly into the floor, keep the elbows straight and move the chest towards the right thigh. Push the right heel towards the floor, look down. Hold the posture for 5 breaths. Exhale, release the left leg to Downward Dog and repeat on the other side.

Precautions: People with diarrhea, headache, high blood pressure or carpel tunnel syndrome should not practice this posture

Benefits: calming the brain and relieving stress; energizing the body; stretching the arms, shoulders, hamstrings and calves; slimming effect on arms and legs; improving digestion, relieving headache, insomnia, back pain and fatigue.

COBRA POSE 1

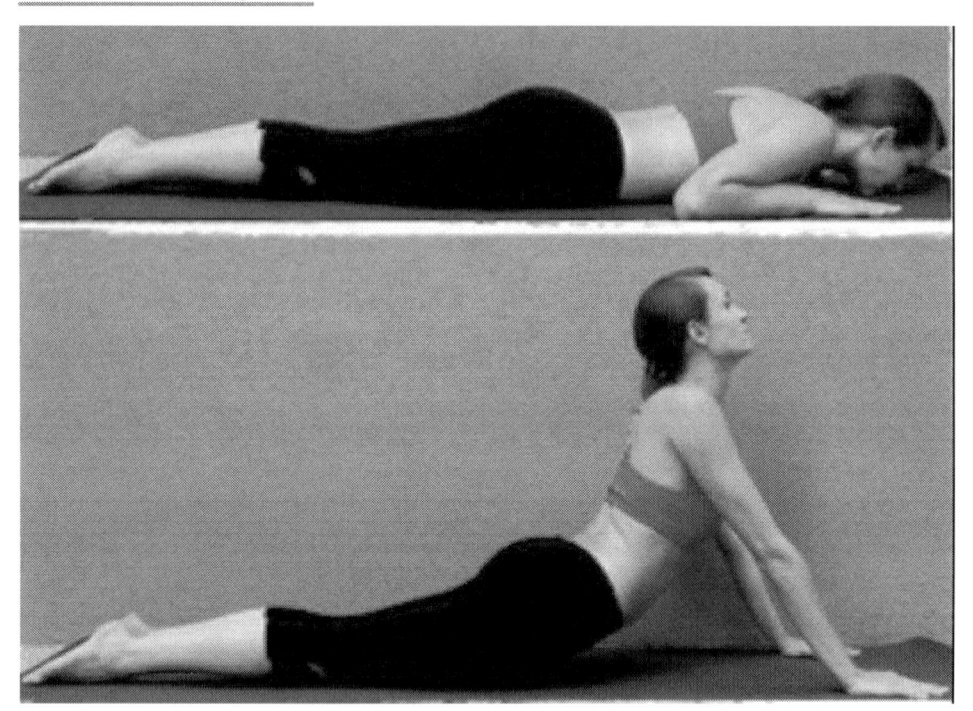

Lay flat on the stomach with the chin resting on the floor, the legs straight, feet together, and the soles of the feet facing upwards. Place the palms next to your ears. Inhale, slide the chest forward and raise first the head, the shoulders, then, straightening the elbows, arch the back. This will lower the hips and the buttocks to the floor. Bend the head to the back and look upward. Relax your shoulders. Hold the pose for 5 breaths. Exhale, slowly bend the elbows, lower the chest and chin on the floor

Precautions: People suffering from peptic ulcer, hernia, intestinal tuberculosis or hyperthyroidism should not practice this asana without consulting it with a doctor

Benefits: removing backache, keeping the spine flexible; alleviating constipation and is beneficial for all abdominal organs, especially the liver and kidneys; strengthening the spine, chest, abdomen, shoulders; firming the buttocks; opening heart and lungs.

COBRA POSE 2

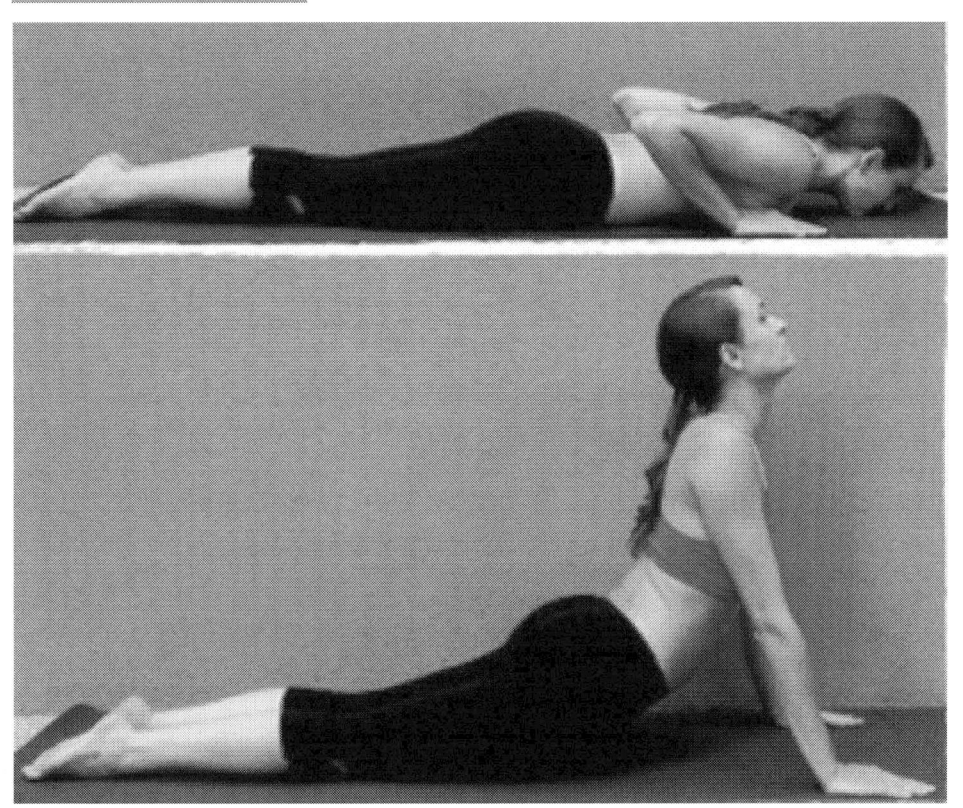

Lay flat on the stomach with the chin resting on the floor, the legs straight, feet together, and the soles of the feet facing upwards. Place the palms next to your chest. Inhale, slide the chest forward and raise first the head, the shoulders, then, straightening the elbows, arch the back. This will lower the hips and the buttocks to the floor. Bend the head to the back and look upward. Relax your shoulders. Hold the pose for 5 breaths. Exhale, slowly bend the elbows, lower the chest and chin on the floor

Precautions: People suffering from peptic ulcer, hernia, intestinal tuberculosis or hyperthyroidism should not practice this asana without consulting it with a doctor

Benefits: removing backache, keeping the spine flexible; alleviating constipation and is beneficial for all abdominal organs, especially the liver and kidneys; strengthening the spine, chest, abdomen, shoulders; firming the buttocks; opening heart and lungs.

COBRA POSE 3

Lay flat on the stomach with the chin resting on the floor, the legs straight, feet together, and the soles of the feet facing upwards. Place the palms next to your waist. Inhale, slide the chest forward and raise first the head, the shoulders, then, straightening the elbows, arch the back. This will raise your hips and upper thighs of the mat. Bend the head to the back and look upward. Relax your shoulders. Hold the pose for 5 breaths. Exhale, slowly bend the elbows, lower the chest and chin on the floor

Precautions: People suffering from peptic ulcer, hernia, intestinal tuberculosis or hyperthyroidism should not practice this asana without consulting it with a doctor

Benefits: removing backache, keeping the spine flexible; alleviating constipation and is beneficial for all abdominal organs, especially the liver and kidneys; strengthening the spine, chest, abdomen, shoulders; firming the buttocks; opening heart and lungs.

HALF BOAT POSE

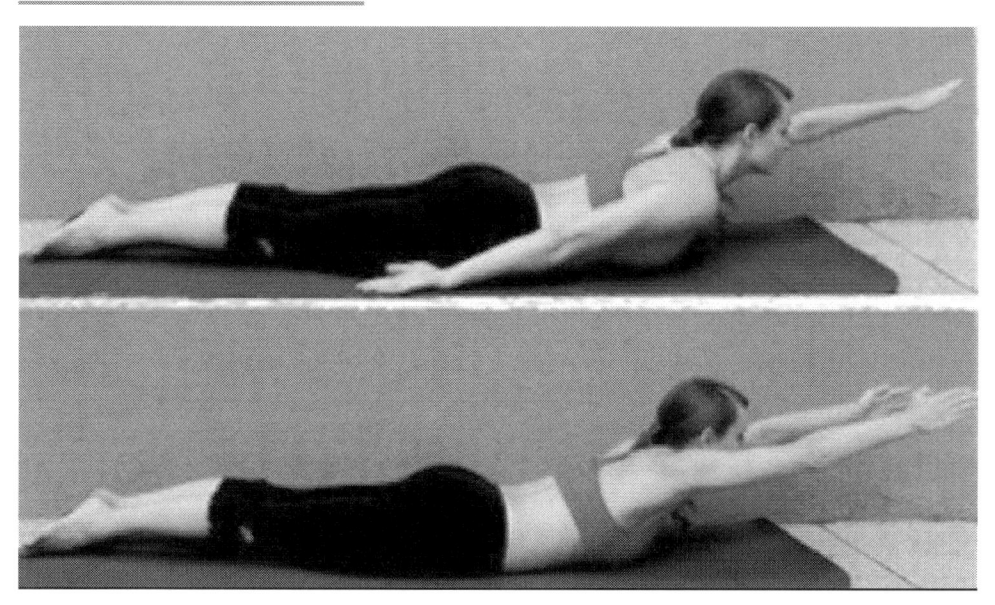

Lay flat on the stomach with the legs and feet together and the soles of the feet facing upwards. Place the arms in front of your body, with the palms facing downward. Inhale, using the back muscles raise your straight hands as high as possible without straining (option: raise only one hand and than change the sides). Keep the feet on the floor, don't raise it up. Hold the pose for 5 breaths. Exhale, slowly lower the legs and hands to the floor. Return to the starting position and relax.

Precautions: People with weak heart, coronary thrombosis, serious back problems, high blood pressure, peptic ulcer, hernia, intestinal tuberculosis and other such conditions should not practice this pose

Benefits: toning and balancing the functioning of the liver, stomach, bowels, and other abdominal organs; tightening the muscles of the buttocks; strengthening the lower and upper back.

BOAT POSE

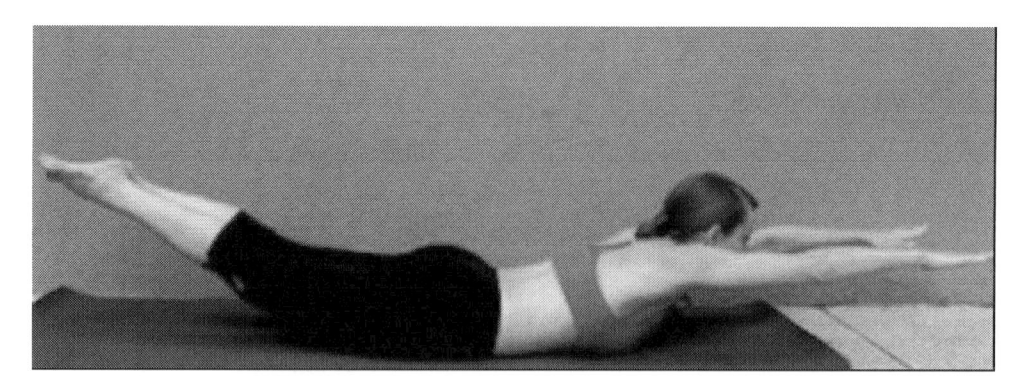

Lay flat on the stomach with the legs and feet together and the soles facing upwards. Place the arms in front of your body, with the palms facing downward. Inhale, using the back muscles raise your both legs and both hands as high as possible without straining, keeping hands and knees straight, legs together. Do not tilt or twist the pelvis. Hold the pose for 5 breaths. Exhale, slowly lower the legs and hands to the floor. Return to the starting position and relax.

Precautions: People with weak heart, coronary thrombosis, serious back problems, high blood pressure, peptic ulcer, hernia, intestinal tuberculosis and other such conditions should not practice this pose

Benefits: toning and balancing the functioning of the liver, stomach, bowels, and other abdominal organs; tightening the muscles of the buttocks; strengthening the lower and upper back; improving posture; relieving stress

HALF LOCUST POSE

Lay flat on the stomach with the legs straight, hands beside the thighs and chin on the floor (you can bring the palms under your thighs for support) Inhale, using the back muscles raise the left leg as high as possible, keeping the other leg straight on the floor. Do not tilt or twist the pelvis, don't raise the chin up. Hold the pose for 5 breaths. Exhale, slowly lower the left leg to the floor. Repeat on the other side.

Precautions: People with weak heart, coronary thrombosis, serious back problems, high blood pressure, peptic ulcer, hernia, intestinal tuberculosis and other such conditions should not practice this pose

Benefits: toning and balancing the functioning of the liver, stomach, bowels, and other abdominal organs; tightening the muscles of the buttocks; strengthening the lower and upper back; improving posture; relieving stress

LOCUST POSE

Lay flat on the stomach with the legs straight and chin on the floor. Bring the palms under your thighs. Inhale, using the back muscles raise your both legs as high as possible, keeping the knees straight. Do not tilt or twist the pelvis, don't raise the chin up. Hold the pose for 5 breaths. Exhale and slowly lower the legs to the floor. Return to the starting position and relax.

Precautions: People with weak heart, coronary thrombosis, serious back problems, high blood pressure, peptic ulcer, hernia, intestinal tuberculosis and other such conditions should not practice this pose

Benefits: toning and balancing the functioning of the liver, stomach, bowels, and other abdominal organs; tightening the muscles of the buttocks; strengthening the lower and upper back; improving posture; relieving stress

BOW POSE

Lay flat on the stomach with the legs 1 foot apart and chin on the floor, bend the knees, grab hold of your ankles and bring the heels close to the buttocks. Inhale, tense the leg muscles and push the feet away from the body. Arch the back, lifting the thighs, chest and head together, keep the arms straight. In the final position the abdomen supports the entire body on the floor. Hold the pose for 5 breaths. Exhale, slowly release the pose and relax.

Precautions: People with weak heart, high blood pressure, hernia, colitis, peptic or duodenal ulcers shouldn't practice this pose. It shouldn't be practiced until at least 3-4 hours after a meal and before sleep as it stimulates the adrenal glands and the sympathetic nervous system.

Benefits: this is the best yoga pose to burn belly fat; it's toning and stretching the entire front of the body, ankles, abdomen, thighs, chest, throat and spine; improving the functioning of the digestive organs; strengthening leg muscles, especially thighs.

CROCKODILE POSE

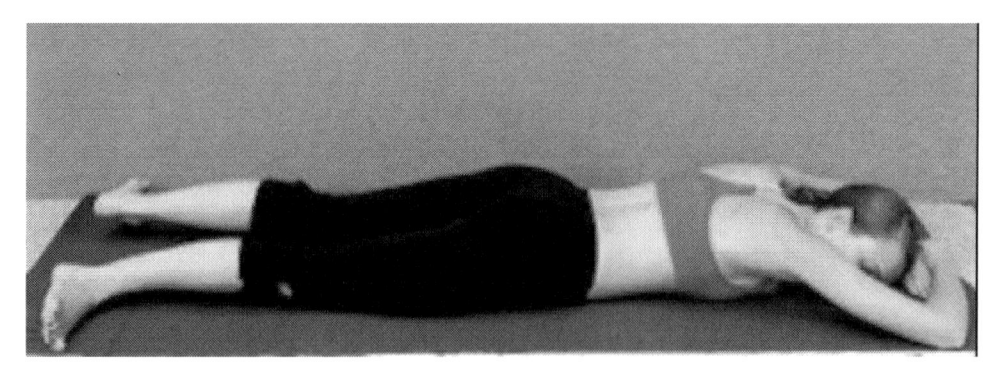

Lay down flat on the stomach. Spread your legs slightly with your feet pointing outwards. Bring your hands to the front and fold your arms. Tilt your head to the side and lay down in this pose to relax your back.

Precautions: People with back conditions such as exaggerated lumbar curve, should not practice this posture if any pain is experienced

Benefits: It's very effective for people suffering from slipped disc, sciatica and certain types of lower back pain. Remaining in this asana for extended periods of time encourages the vertebral column to resume it's normal shape and releases compression of the spinal nerves.

Supine Sequence Poses - Building The Abdominal & Spinal Power

CORPSE POSE

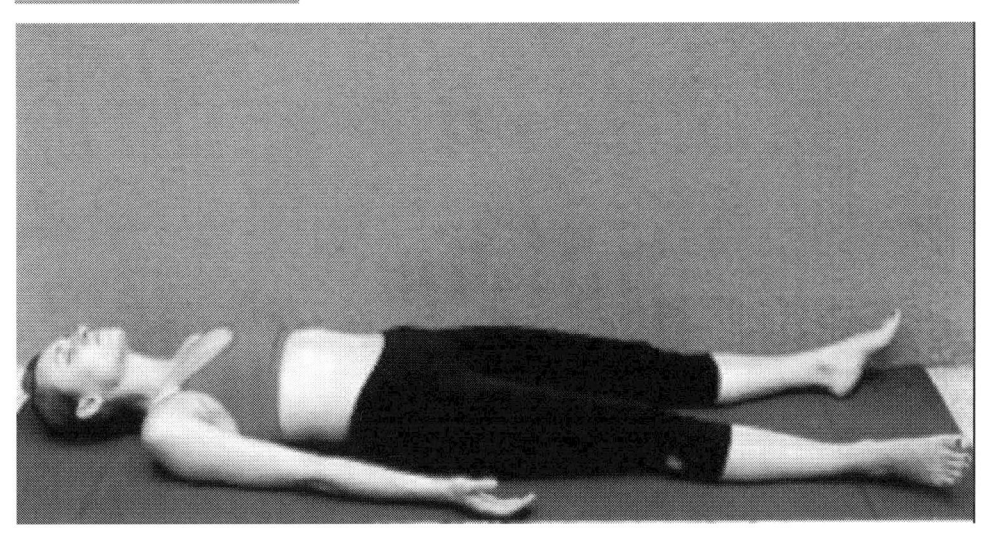

Lay down on your back with the hands away from the body, palms facing upwards. Let the fingers curl-up slightly; don't keep them straight forcefully. Spread your legs slightly apart and close your eyes. Your head and spine should be in straight line, make sure your head won't fall to the side. Relax.

Precautions: None

Benefits: relaxing the whole psycho-physiological system; it can be practiced before the sleep, before, during and after postures, especially after Sun Salutations

ONE LEG RAISED POSE

Lay down on your back with your hands beside the hips, palms facing downwards. Inhale, raise your left leg up to 90 degrees. Keep your legs straight, toes relaxed, don't bend the knee. Gaze up at your toes. Your right leg should remain straight on the floor. Hold the posture for 5 breaths. Exhale, slowly lower your leg down on the floor, keeping the knee straight. Repeat on the other side

Option: If your back is weak, the right leg can be bent with your knee up and foot on the floor

Precautions: People with high blood pressure or serious back problems like sciatica or slipped disc should not perform this posture

Benefits: Strengthening the abdominal muscles, digestive system and lower back; massaging abdominal organs

BOTH LEGS RAISED POSE

Lay down on your back with your hands beside the hips, palms facing downwards. Inhale, raise your both legs up to 90 degrees. Keep your legs straight, toes relaxed, don't bend the knee. Gaze up at your toes. Hold the posture for 5 breaths. Exhale, slowly lower your legs down on the floor, keeping the knees straight. Repeat few times.

Option: If your back is weak, you can bend your knees while raising your both legs up and straighten your legs once they are up in 90 degrees

Precautions: People with high blood pressure or serious back problems like sciatica or slipped disc should not perform this posture

Benefits: Strengthening the abdominal muscles, digestive system and lower back; massaging abdominal organs.

EASY HALF GAS RELEASE POSE

Lay down on your back with your hands beside the hips, palms facing downwards. Inhale, raise the left leg up to 90 degrees. Exhale, grab your left knee or shin, interlock your fingers, bend the knee and bring it to the chest. Keep the right leg straight on the floor. Hold the pose for 5 breaths. Inhale, straighten the knee and raise the left leg up to 90 degrees. Exhale, release the left leg down on the floor. Repeat on the other side

Precautions: People with high blood pressure or serious back problems like sciatica, piles, hernia or slipped disc or those after recent abdominal surgery should not practice this posture

Benefits: loosening and relaxing the spinal vertebrae; massaging the abdomen and digestive organs - a perfect pose for removing wind and constipation; increasing blood circulation in abdominal organs; improving digestion

HALF GAS RELEASE POSE

Lay down on your back with your hands beside the hips, palms facing downwards. Inhale, raise the left leg up to 90 degrees. Exhale, grab your knee or shin, interlock your fingers, bend the knee and bring it to the chest. Inhale, raise your head up and bring the nose or forehead to the knee. Keep the right leg straight on the floor. Hold the pose for 5 breaths. Exhale, release the head on the floor. Inhale, straighten the knee and raise the left leg up to 90 degrees. Exhale, release the left leg down on the floor. Repeat on the other side

Precautions: People with high blood pressure or serious back problems like sciatica, piles, hernia or slipped disc or those after recent abdominal surgery should not practice this posture

Benefits: strengthening the neck and lower back, loosening spinal vertebrae; massaging the abdomen and the digestive organs - a perfect pose for removing wind and constipation; increasing blood circulation in abdominal organs; improving digestion

EASY GAS RELEASE POSE

Lay down on your back with your hands beside the hips, palms facing downwards. Inhale, raise your both legs up to 90 degrees. Exhale, drop your both knees on the chest; hold your knees tightly. Relax the spine and hold the pose for 5 breaths. Inhale, straighten the knees and raise both legs up to 90 degrees. Exhale, release the legs down on the floor.

Precautions: People with high blood pressure or serious back problems like sciatica, piles, hernia or slipped disc or those after recent abdominal surgery should not practice this posture

Benefits: loosening and relaxing the lower back; massaging abdomen and digestive organs - it's a perfect pose for removing wind and constipation; increasing blood circulation in abdominal organs; improving digestion

GAS RELEASE POSE

Lay down on your back with your hands beside the hips, palms facing downwards. Inhale, raise both legs up to 90 degrees. Exhale, drop your both knees on the chest, grab hold of the knees. Inhale, raise your head up and place your chin in between your knees. Hold the pose for 5 breaths. Exhale, release the head on the floor. Inhale, straighten the knees and raise it up to 90 degrees. Exhale, release both legs down on the floor.

Precautions: People with high blood pressure or serious back problems like sciatica, piles, hernia or slipped disc or those after recent abdominal surgery should not practice this posture

Benefits: loosening and relaxing the lower back; massaging abdomen and digestive organs - it's a perfect pose for removing wind and constipation; increasing blood circulation in abdominal organs; improving digestion

BRIDGE POSE 1

Lay down on your back with your hands beside the hips, palms facing downwards. Bend the knees, placing the soles of the feet flat on the floor hip width apart. Inhale, raise the buttocks and arch the back upward. Raise the chest and navel and high as possible without straining. Push the chest up towards the chin and head. In the final position, the body is supported by the head, neck, shoulders, arms and feet. Hold this pose for 5 breaths. Exhale, lower the body to the starting position.

Precautions: People suffering from peptic or duodenal ulcers, abdominal hernia or neck injuries should not practice this pose

Benefits: relieving stress, backache, headache and fatigue; stimulating abdominal organs, colon, lungs and thyroid glands, improving digestion; rejuvenating tired legs; slimming effect on thighs and buttocks

BRIDGE POSE 2

Lay down on your back with your hands beside the hips, palms facing downwards. Bend the knees, placing the soles of the feet flat on the floor hip width apart. Inhale, raise the buttocks and heels and arch the back upward. Raise the chest and navel and high as possible without straining. Push the chest up towards the chin and head. In the final position, the body is supported by the head, neck, shoulders, arms and toes. Hold this pose for 5 breaths. Exhale, lower the body to the starting position.

Precautions: People suffering from peptic or duodenal ulcers, abdominal hernia or neck injuries should not practice this pose

Benefits: relieving stress, backache, headache and fatigue; stimulating abdominal organs, colon, lungs and thyroid glands, improving digestion; rejuvenating tired legs; slimming effect on thighs and buttocks

BRIDGE POSE 3

Lay down on your back with your hands beside the hips, palms facing downwards. Bend the knees, placing the soles of the feet flat on the floor hip width apart. Inhale, raise the buttocks, heels and left leg up and arch the back upward. Raise the chest and navel as high as possible without straining. Push the chest up towards the chin and head. In the final position, the body is supported by the head, neck, shoulders, arms and right leg. Hold this pose for 5 breaths. Exhale, and repeat with the other leg.

Precautions: People suffering from peptic or duodenal ulcers, abdominal hernia or neck injuries should not practice this pose

Benefits: relieving stress, backache, headache and fatigue; stimulating abdominal organs, colon, lungs and thyroid glands, improving digestion; rejuvenating tired legs; slimming effect on thighs and buttocks

EASY LOWER BACK TWIST

Lay down on your back with your hands beside the hips, palms facing downwards. Inhale, bend the left knee, grab the knee with the right palm. Stretch the left hand on the floor on the shoulder level. Exhale, bring the left bent knee to the right side, touch the knee to the floor, keep the right leg straight. Twist the head and look to the left side at your palm. Hold the pose for 5 breaths. Inhale, straighten the head and raise the knee. Exhale, release the left leg straight on the floor. Repeat on the other side

Precautions: People with serious back problems like sciatica, piles, hernia or slipped disc should be careful with this posture

Benefits: loosening up muscles and relaxing the spinal vertebrae; twisting the lower back relieves tension in this area; lowering the blood pressure; perfect pose to practice at the end of the Yoga session to relieve any tension in the lower back.

LOWER BACK TWIST

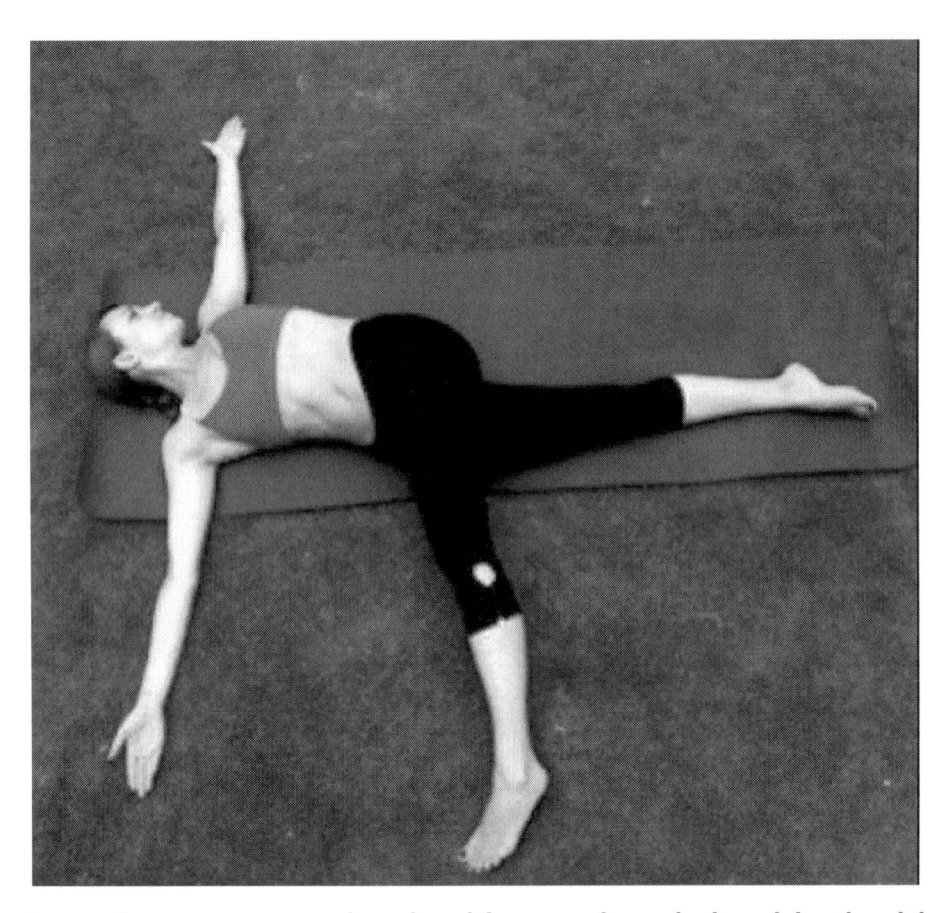

Lay down on your back with your hands beside the hips, palms facing downwards. Inhale, raise the left leg up to 90 degrees, stretch both hands to the sides on the shoulder level. Exhale, bring the left straight leg to the right side, touch the toes to the floor, keep the right leg straight. Twist the head and look to the left side at your palm. Hold the pose for 5 breaths. Inhale, straighten the head and raise the leg up to 90 degrees. Exhale, release the left leg straight on the floor. Repeat on the other side.

Precautions: People with serious back problems like sciatica, piles, hernia or slipped disc should be careful with this posture

Benefits: loosening up muscles and relaxing the spinal vertebrae; twisting the lower back relieves tension in this area; lowering the blood pressure; perfect pose to practice at the end of the Yoga session to relieve any tension in the lower back.

Closing Sequence Poses - Relaxing The Body & Calming The Mind

FACE PALMING

Sit down in any meditative pose (Easy Meditation Pose, Half Lotus Pose or Lotus Pose). Close your eyes, breathe normally, relax. While keeping your eyes closed, bring your palms together and start rubbing the palms until they feel warm. Slowly palm your eyes, avoid applying pressure on the eye balls. Keep your eyes covered for few seconds. Release the hands, rub the palms one more time. Palm the cheeks and hold it for few seconds. Release the hands, rub the palms one more time. Palm the neck and hold it for few seconds. Release the hands, keep your eyes closed for few more seconds, then slowly open the eyes and release the meditative pose.

Benefits: relaxing and revitalizing the eye, face and neck muscles; stimulating the liquid that flows between the cornea and the lens of the eye; aiding the correction of defective vision; bringing relaxation to the entire body; perfect practice for the beginning and end of a Yoga session

MOUNTAIN POSE

Sit down in any meditative pose (Easy Meditation Pose, Half Lotus Pose or Lotus Pose). Inhale, raise your both hands up over the head, interlock the fingers, palms facing upwards. Stretch your whole body. Look forward and hold the stretch for few seconds. Exhale, release the hands on the floor.

Precautions: People suffering from sciatica or weak or injured knees should not perform this posture

Benefits: strengthening the abdominal muscles, digestive system and spine muscles; relieving tension from the lower back; relaxing the whole body

SIDE MOUNTAIN POSE

Sit down in any meditative pose (Easy Meditation Pose, Half Lotus Pose or Lotus Pose) Inhale, raise your both hands up over the head, interlock the fingers, palms facing upwards. Stretch your whole body up. Exhale, bend the trunk and outstretched arms to the left side. Look to the right and up, hold the pose for few seconds. Inhale, center the hands and trunk and repeat on the other side

Precautions: People suffering from sciatica, weak or injured knees or after recent abdominal surgery should not perform this posture.

Benefits: strengthening the abdominal muscles, digestive system and spine muscles; gently stretching and trimming the waist; relieving tension from the lower back; relaxing the whole body

SURRENDER POSE

Sit down in any meditative pose (Easy Meditation Pose, Half Lotus Pose or Lotus Pose). Inhale, raise your both hands up over the head, interlock the fingers, palms facing upwards. Stretch your whole body up. Exhale, bend your trunk forward and bring the hands in front on the floor. Try to touch the forehead to the floor and stretch the spine. Hold the pose for few seconds and breathe normally. Inhale, slowly raise the trunk and hands up, go back to the sitting pose. Exhale; release the hands and meditative pose.

Precautions: People suffering from sciatica or weak or injured knees should not perform this posture

Benefits: strengthening abdominal muscles, digestive system and spine muscles; pressure on the abdominal organs stimulates digestion; relieving tension from the lower back and arms; relaxing the whole body.

Have a nice time

Printed in Great Britain
by Amazon